Spiritual Woman

Nurturing Your Soul

HARRIET HODGSON

North Carolina

Spiritual Woman: Nurturing Your Soul

Some of the content in this book was previously published by Harriet Hodgson in December 2010 with Grief Illustrated Press under the title The Spiritual Woman: Quotes to Refresh and Sustain Your Soul.

Published in the United States by WriteLife Publishing
(an imprint of Boutique of Quality Books Publishing Company, Inc.)
www.writelife.com

9781608083053 (p)
9781608083060 (e)

Library of Congress Control Number: 2025944819

Book design by Robin Krauss, www.bookformatters.com
Cover design by Rebecca Lown, www.rebeccalowndesign.com
Editor: Andrea Vande Vorde

Praise for *Spiritual Woman* and Harriet Hodgson

"*Spiritual Woman: Nurturing Your Soul* will be a welcome companion for each woman who discovers it. Harriet Hodgson has a gift for shaping the ordinary and familiar things around us into unique creations. She offers, in a new way, quotations and practices familiar to many of us. This is her gift to us for nurturing the deep well-spring, often hidden from others and from ourselves, that makes each one of us unique and lovable. The rapidity of changes is American culture makes Harriet's insights and recommendations both timely and timeless."

— Carolyn Stickney Beck, Ph.D.

"In *Spiritual Woman,* Harriet Hodgson shows her ability to cut through the chaff to find the golden kernel inside. Her simple, common-sense introduction to including meditation into our lives makes the formidable seem achievable. Her list of funny, spiritual, and poignant quotes helps us begin the process of 'nurturing our souls.' A lovely book."

— Judith Gunnon

"Harriet Hodgson, in her book *Spiritual Woman,* shares her multifaceted ways of coping with the vissitudes of life. Throughout history, religions have provided solace from prayer, rituals, and commandments. . . . Harriet's quotes offer food for thought and solace for all who need it. Who does not? There are times in our lives when we all do. Each of us has to find our own way, be it prayer, meditations, music, art, or science. Women must learn to take care of themselves physically and emotionally. This book helps us do that. Harriet's message of compassion and self-care is for all, women and men. It's a winner!"

— Dr. Bani Mahadeva

"The title of this book surely matches its contents, and it definitely nurtures one's soul. One would not have to consider themselves spiritual to benefit from this book. It will help you relax and just help you feel better. A great book to keep near you for inspiration. I truly loved *Spiritual Woman*!"

— Helen Staley

"*Spiritual Woman* is a book that should appeal to women of all ages. The meditation pathways were informative, and the many quotes allowed me to reach my 'inner spirit' in ways I had not thought of before. I recommend this book to all, even those who find 'spiritual' a word not in their lexicon. They may be surprised, *Spiritual Woman* is a delightful book."

— Margaret S. Freel, RN, MSN

"*Spiritual Woman* guided me gently from the beginning to end. I felt like Harriet had invited me for a chat and a cuppa. She has the ability to share depth and challenges and directions for the reader to freely choose from. The key is flexibility. The quotes will help you nurture yourself and yes, move foward. I can see this book with well-worn pages, written marks, and sticky notes, as women start a healing journey of the soul. A good choice for special book discussions."

— Donna Hazelwood

"As a female chaplain, I found Harriet Hodgson's meditation approach to be both insightful and refreshingly pragmatic for everyone. Kudos to her! This is definitely a book worth reading!"

— Rev. Inetta A. Reddell, MA, MDIV, MA Bioethics, BCC
President, Association of Professional Chaplains

Contents

Part I

Your Inner Spirit

Women are very aware of their emotions. Perhaps this comes from carrying babies in our wombs, giving birth to new life, adopting children, caring for loved ones and wiggly pets, pursuing our careers, and helping in our communities. The women of the world have many things in common, and we need to remember this.

Like the beads of a necklace, different experiences come together to form a woman's life. Sometimes we are so happy we think we will burst. Other times, we are so burdened we think we will collapse. There are days when getting out of bed is a struggle. As we mature, an important truth becomes clear: A woman's soul helps her meet the challenges of life.

What is the soul? The word "soul" refers to all the nonphysical things that make us who we are: our thinking, personality, intuition, values, ethics, humor, talent, conversation, social skills, memories, and dreams. A woman's soul is her inner truth.

Your soul is a rudder that steers you in various directions. Just as plants can't grow without regular care, neither can your soul. You need time, solitude, and quiet to do this, things that are hard to find in today's world. Even if you regularly care for your soul, you may lose touch with it for a while. You may even feel like you've lost control of your life.

At those times, some of your thoughts may be negative, others positive, and others unclear. When that happens, it is time to nurture your soul. This book is filled with tools you can use to nurture your soul and one of those tools is meditation. I find meditation to be comforting and helpful. The quiet slows my mind and my breathing. Then too, the quiet comforts me. When I meditate, I'm nurturing my soul.

Because meditation works so well for nurturing our souls, I've dedicated several pages of this book to the subject. There are several styles of meditation which will help you individualize it for your life and your soul.

In "Meditation: Focusing Your Mind To Achieve Stress Reduction," an article published on the Mayo Clinic website, Mayo defines meditation as "a complementary and alternative medicine practice that falls under the category of mind-body techiques."

I've found meditation to be beneficial in many ways:

- self-knowledge
- identifying feelings
- awareness of your strengths
- awareness of your weaknesses
- seeing the causes of problems
- finding solutions to problems
- developing self-control
- broader view of life
- understanding your life purpose
- reviewing your goals
- setting new goals
- coming up with creative ideas
- developing your personal truth
- gratefulness for the things you have
- developing wisdom
- a sense of peace
- reverence for life

How you meditate is a personal decision. For some, prayer is a form of meditation. Others meditate by sitting in a quiet place and letting their thoughts wander. Still others meditate by focusing their mind on one topic. No matter which type of meditation you choose, meditation takes time, and you need to give yourself this time.

I use meditation to slow my creative mind, which is going all the time. By closing my eyes, slowing my breathing, and saying a short prayer, I give my mind a brief rest. When I meditate, I go through several steps. First, I tell myself that I have the ability to slow my mind. I close my eyes and slow my breathing. Then I visualize a blank, gray television screen. Often, I focus on one word, such as love. After meditating and breathing slowly for 15-20 minutes, I say the short prayer I have included at the back of this book and I resume my day.

As Daniel Goleman, PhD, explains in *Working with Emotional Intelligence*, "In the rush and pressure of our work days, our needs are preoccupied by the stream of thought—planning the next thing, immersion in our present talk, preoccupation with things undone . . . Our feelings are always with us, but we are too seldom with them."

Why should you refresh your soul? Refreshing your soul is an important part of a balanced life. When you care for your soul, you create a well-spring of strength you may tap into again and again. As you read the quotes in the part of this book titled "Daily Words," keep in mind that religion and spirituality are not the same.

Religion is a community view of life, with specific rituals and beliefs usually stated in doctrine. Spirituality is an individual view of life, your innermost thoughts, and the actions you take on them.

Though this book contains quotes from people affiliated with various faiths, it does not represent or endorse any specific religion.

Each quote has been chosen to keep you moving forward in life. You may use the quotes in several ways. The quotes may serve as a preface to yoga and walking. Before mealtime, you may read a quote aloud. Support groups may use the quotations for group discussions. You may choose a quote and meditate about it. Even better, jot down a quote on a piece of sticky paper and post it where you'll see it often.

Caring for your soul is an ongoing challenge. In fact, BettyClare Moffatt, author of *Soulwork: Clearing the Mind, Opening the Heart, Replenishing the Spirit,* thinks caring for the soul is lifetime work. "Soulwork is living with conscious grace and wisdom, whatever your circumstances, and using all that you are—body, mind, emotion, and spirit—in your ever-changing, individual dance of life," she writes.

Your dance of life takes place at a challenging time in history. The world has become a noisy, fast-paced, scary place. Some women hardly have time to hear their thoughts or put mental periods on their sentences. Don't feel guilty about taking the time to nurture your soul, because it will benefit you greatly. You are worth the time and effort.

Nurturing your soul is a necessity, something you do for yourself, and those you love. How you approach each day is a glimpse of your soul, something personal and unique and sacred.

Part 2

Before You Begin

I compiled the quotations in Part 5, "Daily Words," to inspire women of all ages and stages of life. As you read the quotes, the image of a spiritual woman begins to take shape. By the end of the book, this image is virtually complete.

While the image may not entirely fit you, the sparks of spirituality connect you with the life you're living now. You may be starting a new career, growing an established career, nearing retirement, or already retired and seeking new horizons. Wherever you are in life, each quote nurtures your soul, and that's good for you, family, friends, colleagues, and strangers you have yet to meet.

Still, upbeat quotations don't ensure happiness. Think of your spirituality as a form of self-care, something that needs nurturing. You do this by taking forward steps and connecting with other women. Whether these women are your age, years older, or far younger, it doesn't matter. We're all in this world together.

We can nurture one another by listening attentively, sharing reliable information, swapping books, and giving hugs. I've found that asking permission before you hug someone is a thoughtful thing to do. *Spiritual Woman* helps you tend to your soul, and that leads to a rich, fulfilling life. Savor it.

Part 3

Eight Meditation Pathways

The word meditation means "a peaceful mind." On their website mayoclinic.org, the Mayo Clinic provides the following information about meditation:

There are four main pathways to meditation: intellect, emotions, body, and action. These major pathways may be divided into many sub-pathways. Here are some to consider.

1. **Empty Mind:** This type of meditation involves clearing thoughts from your mind. You may sit in the lotus position while you meditate.
2. **Focused:** With focused meditation, you think about a specific idea or concept, such as giving or gratefulness.
3. **Mindfulness:** This type of meditation comes from Buddhism. As you meditate, you are aware of your breathing and thoughts. You are in the moment.
4. **Qi Gong:** This path brings together yoga, tai chi, focused breathing, and focused attention.
5. **Sufi Walking or Dancing:** Originally from medieval Islam, this path involves walking or dancing rhythmically while chanting.
6. **Tai Chi:** This path came from China and was originally a martial art. Tai Chi is a series of slow, circular postures combined with deep breathing.

7. **Yoga:** This is a series of various postures. As you assume these postures, you pay special attention to the inhaling and exhaling of your breath. Yoga also promotes flexibility and strength.
8. **Walking Meditation:** As you walk slowly, you are aware of your body, the movement of your legs and feet, and breathing. You also focus your thoughts on a specific topic.

I have used three of these pathways: empty mind, focused, and mindfulness. Of the three, I don't have a favorite and alternate the pathways instead. Sometimes I use the empty mind pathway as a prelude to focused meditation. When I do this, I focus on one word, such as love or giving or family. Often, I use the mindfulness pathway because I can do it anywhere and everywhere.

Mindfulness can be a challenging pathway because it requires total concentration and observation. The best way to find a pathway that suits you is to try it a few times. Was the pathway easy for you? How did you feel afterward? Would you use this pathway again?

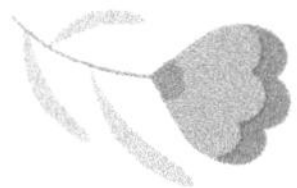

References

Goleman, Daniel. *Working With Emotional Intelligence*. New York: Bantam Books. 1998.

"Meditation: Focusing Your Mind to Achieve Stress Reduction." Mayo Clinic. Sept. 5, 2021, http://www.mayoclinic.com/health/meditation/HQ01070

Moffatt, BettyClare. *Soulwork: Clearing the Mind, Opening the Heart, and Replenishing the Spirit*. Wildcat Canyon Press. 1994.

Part 4

Meditation Tips

For me, meditation isn't like flipping a switch. It takes me about fifteen minutes to prepare myself. When I do this, I sit in a comfortable chair, picture a blank television screen in my mind, and slow my breathing. These meditation tips come from research and experience. The tips helped me (especially the experience ones) and may help you.

- Learn about the various approaches to meditation.
- Choose a type of meditation that works best for you.
- If the type you tried doesn't work, try another one.
- Keep at it, even if your first meditation sessions are not as successful as you hoped.
- Meditate regularly. Early morning or just before bedtime may work for you.
- Eliminate all background noise if possible.
- Sit or stand in a comfortable position.
- Relax your body.
- Repeat a word or phrase (mantra) to help you relax.
- Clear your mind of clutter.

- Focus on your breathing.
- Keep a journal.
- Participate in a retreat to learn more about meditation.
- Try to apply what you learn from meditation to daily life.

Part 5

Daily Words

Words fascinate me. In case you're wondering, I keep an ongoing mental list of favorite words: love, tender, surprise, gift, gentle, heartfelt, true, blessed, and more. I keep adding words to my favorites list. Quotes fascinate me just as much as individual words, and like the words list, I have my favorites.

I enjoy quotes by poet and priest John O'Donohue, poet Robert Frost (one of my all-time favorite poets), and those who make me smile, including artist/illustrator Mary Englebreit, who thinks we should "Bloom where you are planted." As Mary suggested, I'm doing my best to bloom, and you probably are too.

Because I'm always ready for a good laugh, quotes that make me laugh get my attention immediately. I tend to remember these quotes and keep laughing at them.

Even if I'm familiar with a quote, and have read it often, I read it again and receive the same joy from it. One quote, the well-know Irish blessing, is such a forite I memorized it.

May the road rise up to meet you.
May the wind always be at your back.
May the sunshine warm upon your face,
the rain fall soft upon your fields, and,
until we meet again,
may God hold you in the palm of his hand.

Though I have English and German heritage (not a smidge of Irish), many days have started with me reading the Irish prayer aloud. It's beautiful. It's touching. And it applies to everyone.

Words are stored in the mind and often repeat themselves, which can be a blessing or an annoyance. You'll most likely find quotes that become your favorites among those listed on the following pages. When you do, copy a quote and display it on the refrigerator, bathroom mirror, or somewhere that you can see it every day. Leave it there as long as you want, and when the time comes, replace the quote with another. You may also want to copy a quote for a friend and give it to that person for comfort.

Before you start reading the quotes on the following pages, I suggest you tab pages that contain your favorite quotes or put a checkmark by them with a pencil. Or use a highlighter and highlight them for easy access. Read these quotes repeatedly. Let the words seep into your soul.

1

"We are not born all at once, but by bits. The body first, and the spirit later; and the birth and growth of the spirit, in those who are attentive to their own inner life . . ."

— *Mary Antin*

2

"Life is no brief candle to me. It is a sort of splendid torch which I have got a hold of for the moment, and I want to make it burn as brightly as possible before handing it on to future generations."

— *George Bernard Shaw*

3

"Precious Lord, take my hand, lead me on, help me stand."

— *Thomas A. Dorsey*

4

"Let me never be afraid of endings or beginnings. Teach me to embrace all of life with joy."

— *Helen Lesman*

5

"Be kind to your mind. Clean it out and make it your friend, your resting place, your home."

— *Hugh Prather*

6

"What a happy and holy fashion it is that those who love one another should rest on the same pillow."

— *Nathaniel Hawthorne*

7

"A friend is a gift you give yourself."

— *Robert Louis Stevenson*

8

"May all that is unlived in you
Blossom into a future
Graced with love."

— *John O'Donohue*

9

"We choose our joys and sorrows long before we experience them."

— *Kahlil Gibran*

10

"Those who wish to sing always find a song."

— *Swedish Proverb*

11

"I feel the greatest gift we can give to anybody
is the gift of our honest self."

— Fred Rogers

12

"It takes a lot of courage to show your dreams to someone else."

— Erma Bombeck

13

"Every age sort has its own history. History is really the stories that
we retell to ourselves to make them relevant to every age.
So we put our own values and our own spin on it."

— Terry Jones

14

"You don't choose your family. They are God's gift to you,
as you are to them."

— Desmond Tutu

15

"Life is uncharted territory. It reveals its story
one moment at a time."

— Leo Buscaglia

16

"Grant me intention, purpose, and design—
That's near enough for me to the divine."

— Robert Frost

17

"We have a hunger of the mind which asks for knowledge of all around us, and the more we gain, the more is our desire; the more we see, the more we are capable of seeing."

— Maria Mitchell

18

"We cannot really love anybody with whom we never laugh."

— Agnes Repplier

19

"Only I can change my life. No one can do it for me."

— Carol Burnett

20

"I know God will not give me anything I can't handle. I just wish He didn't trust me so much."

— Mother Teresa

21

"Solitary trees, if they grow at all, grow strong."

— Winston Churchill

22

"We are not human beings on a spiritual journey.
We are spiritual beings on a human journey."

— Stephen Covey

23

"We never become truly spiritual by sitting down and wishing to become so. You must undertake something so great that you cannot accomplish it unaided."

— Phillips Brooks

24

"Blessed is the man [woman] who finds out which way God is moving and then gets going in the same direction."

— Author Unknown

25

"Tears heighten our awareness of self and others."

— Jeffrey A. Kottler

26

"I wait. And that has been a big lesson to be willing, to be still with myself, and trust myself and my higher power to help me make the right decision."

— *Oprah Winfrey*

27

"Let us not look back in anger or forward in fear, but around in awareness."

— *James Thurber*

28

"A religious awakening which does not awaken the sleeper to love has roused him [or her] in vain."

— *Jessamyn West*

29

"Let there be peace on earth, and let it begin with me."

— *Sy Miller and Jill Jackson*

30

"I love people. I love my family, my children . . . but inside myself is a place where I live all alone and that's where you renew your springs that never dry up."

— *Pearl S. Buck*

31

"Solitude gives birth to the original in us, to beauty, unfamiliar and perilous—to poetry."

— Sigmund Freud

32

"The personal life deeply lived always expands into truths beyond itself."

— Anaïs Nin

33

"How many cares one loses when one decides not to be something but to be someone."

— Coco Chanel

34

"The great thing about getting older is that you don't lose all the other ages you've been."

— Madeleine L'Engle

35

"Character— the willingness to accept responsibility for one's own life— is the source from which self respect springs."

— Joan Didion

36

"Love and kindness are never wasted. They always make a difference. They bless the one who receives them, and they bless you, the giver."

— *Barbara De Angelis*

37

"The world is round and the place which may seem like the end may also be the beginning."

— *Ivy Baker Priest*

38

"Faith is not belief. Belief is passive. Faith is active."

— *Edith Hamilton*

39

"Character cannot be developed in ease and quiet. Only through the experience of trial and suffering can the soul be strengthened, vision cleared, ambition inspired, and success achieved."

— *Helen Keller*

40

"Music was my refuge. I could crawl into the space between the notes and curl back to my loneliness."

— *Maya Angelou*

41

"You cannot dream yourself into character;
you must hammer and forge yourself one."

— James A. Froude

42

"It's not whether you get knocked down,
it's whether you get back up."

— Vince Lombardi

43

"In out-of-the places of the heart,
Where your thoughts never think to wander
This beginning has been quietly forming,
Waiting until you were ready to emerge."

— John O'Donohue

44

"The truth is that our finest moments are most likely to occur when we are feeling deeply uncomfortable, unhappy, or unfulfilled. For it is only in such moments, propelled by our discomfort, that we are likely to step out of our ruts and start reaching for different ways or truer answers."

— M. Scott Peck

45

"Thank you, God for this good life and forgive us if we do not love it enough."

— Garrison Keillor

46

"You need chaos in your soul to give birth to a dancing star."

— Friedrich Nietzsche

47

"I am always doing that which I can not do, in order that I may learn how to do it."

— Pablo Picasso

48

"Do not rely completely on any other human being, however dear. We meet all of life's greatest tests alone."

— Agnes Campbell Macphail

49

"If you're not failing every now and again, it's a sign you're not doing anything very innovative."

— Woody Allen

50

"You have at your disposal a foolproof guidance system to navigate your way through life. This system, which consists of your own feelings, lets you know whether you are off track and headed toward unhappiness and conflict– or on track, headed toward peace of mind."

– Richard Carlson

51

"There is a great difference between worry and concern. A worried person sees a problem, and a concerned person solves a problem."

– Harold Stephens

52

"As life grows briefer, I must make it grow deeper."

– Michel de Montaigne

53

"Never give up, for that is just the place and time that the tide will turn."

– Harriet Beecher Stowe

54

"Trouble is only opportunity in work clothes."

– Henry J. Kaiser

55

"To keep a journal of self-awareness allows you to be an active leader in your own life, to learn from experience in ways that would be nearly impossible without the commitment to reflective and active writing."

— Christina Baldwin

56

"I didn't really become a complete adult until I had the freedom to accept who I am and keep growing."

— Doris Roberts

57

"Each friend represents a world in us, a world possibility not born until they arrive, and it is only by this meaning that a new world is born."

— Anaïs Nin

58

"I believe you are your work. Don't trade the stuff of your life, time, for nothing more than dollars. That's a rotten bargain."

— Rita Mae Brown

59

"We need quiet time to examine our lives openly and honestly . . . spending quiet time alone gives your mind an opportunity to renew itself and create order."

— Susan L. Taylor

60

"It is never too late to be what you might have been."

— George Eliot

61

"I have a very modulated way of dealing with my anger. I have always tried to understand the other person and invariably I've discovered that somebody who rubs you the wrong way has been rubbed the wrong way many times."

— Fred Rogers

62

"Life isn't a matter of milestones, but of moments."

— Rose Kennedy

63

"If you as parents cut corners, your children will too. If you live, they will too. If you spend all your money on yourselves and tithe no portion of it for charities, colleges, churches, synagogues, and civic causes, your children won't either."

— Marian Wright Edelman

64

"A person starts to live when he can live outside himself."

— Albert Einstein

65

"You play the hand you're dealt. I think the game's worthwhile."

— Christopher Reeve

66

"In the beauty of nature lies the spirit of hope."

— Author Unknown

67

"I go to nature to be soothed and healed,
and to have my senses put in tune once more."

— John Burroughs

68

"Let's be grateful for those who give us happiness; they are the charming gardeners who make our soul bloom."

— Marcel Proust

69

"Celebrate the happiness that friends are always giving.
Make every day a holiday and celebrate just living!"

— Amanda Bradley

70

"If you love the life you live, you will live a life of love."

— Author Unknown

71

"Nothing you do for children is ever wasted."

— Garrison Keillor

72

"Laughter is the corrective force which prevents us from becoming cranks."

— Henri Bergson

73

"You can't change what you don't acknowledge."

— Phil McGraw

74

"You are responsible, forever, for what you have tamed.
You are responsible for your own rose."

— Antoine de Saint-Euxpery

75

"When I was young I said to God, 'God, tell me the mystery of the universe.' But God answered, 'That knowledge is for me alone.' So I said, 'God, tell me the mystery of the peanut.' Then God said, 'Well, George, that's more nearly your size.'"

— George Washington Carver

76

"Intuition is a spiritual faculty and does not explain, but simply points the way."

— Joyce Brothers

77

"You have to sniff out joy. Keep your nose to the joy trail."

— Buffy Sainte-Marie

78

"Life happens at the level of events, not words."

— *Alfred Adler*

79

"Character consists of what you do on the third and fourth tries."

— *James A. Michener*

80

"Put your ear down close to your soul and listen hard."

— *Anne Sexton*

81

"And finally I twist my heart round again, so that the bad is on the outside and the good is on the inside, and keep on trying to find a way of becoming what I would like to be, and could be, if there weren't any other people living in the world."

— *Anne Frank*

82

"It is my heart that makes songs, not I."

— *Sara Teasdale*

83

"Self-awareness offers a sure rudder for keeping our career decision in harmony with our deepest values."

— Daniel Goleman

84

"Let us realize that the privilege to work is a gift, that power to work is a blessing, that love of work is success."

— David O. McKay

85

"When wealth is lost, nothing is lost; when health is lost, something is lost; when character is lost, all is lost."

— Billy Graham

86

"May the road rise up to meet you. May the wind always be at your back. May the sun shine warm upon your face,
the rain fall soft upon your fields, and, until we meet again,
may God hold you in the palm of his hand."

— Irish Blessing

87

"It is by not always thinking of yourself, if you can manage it, that you might somehow be happy. Until you make room in your life for someone as important as yourself, you will always be searching and lost."

— Richard Bach

88

"When I started counting my blessings, my whole life turned around."

— Willie Nelson

89

"I stood at the crossroads and fate came to meet me."

— Liz Greene

90

"When you educate a man you educate an individual, but when you educate a woman you educate a nation."

–Johnnetta B. Cole

91

"Being a full-time mother is one of the highest salaried jobs . . . since the payment is pure love."

— Mildred B. Vermont

92

"If you don't like something, change it. If you can't change it, change your attitude. Don't complain."

— Maya Angelou

93

"Certain thoughts are prayers. There are moments when, whatever be the attitude of the body, the soul is on its knees."

— Victor Hugo

94

"Hurrying and worrying are not the same as strength."

— African Proverb

95

"The thing always happens that you really believe in; and the belief in a thing makes it happen."

— Frank Lloyd Wright

96

"As Daddy said, life is 95% anticipation."

— Gloria Swanson

97

"We must deliberately call to mind the joys of our journey.
Perhaps we should try to write down the blessings of one day.
We might begin; we could never end; there are not
pens or paper enough in all the world."

— George F. Butterick

98

"Silence is more musical than any song."

— Christina Rossetti

99

"We must be willing to let go of the life we have planned,
so as to accept the life that is waiting for us."

— Joseph Campbell

100

"Hanging on to resentment is letting someone you despise
live rent-free in your head."

— Ann Landers

101

"When you carry out acts of kindness you get a wonderful feeling
inside. It is as though something inside your body responds
and says, 'Yes, this is how I ought to feel.'"

— Rabbi Harold Kushner

102

"One of the goals of a spiritual life and one of the requirements of inner peace is to love unconditionally."

— *Richard Carlson*

103

"Truth is tough. It will not break like a bubble, at a touch, nay, you may kick it about all day like a football, and it will be round and full at evening."

— *Oliver Wendell Holmes*

104

"We're asked to be Superwoman . . . All I can tell you is that I believe it's a lot easier to write books while bringing up kids than to bring up kids while working nine to five plus housekeeping."

— *Ursula K. Le Guin*

105

"December stillness, crossed by twilight roads,
Teach me to travel far and bear my loads."

— *Siegfried Sassoon*

106

"To live with fear and not be afraid is the final test of maturity."

— *Edward Weeks*

107

"Tough times never last but tough people do."

— Robert Schuller

108

"Be aware of wonder. Live a balanced life—learn some and think some and draw and paint and sing and dance and play and work every day some."

— Robert Fulghum

109

"When I took the leap, I had faith I would find a net; instead, I learned I could fly."

— John Calvi

110

"If you don't concentrate, you'll end up on your rear."

— Tai Babilonia

111

"Too often we underestimate the power of a touch, a smile, a kind word, a listening ear, an honest compliment, or the smallest act of caring, all of which have the potential to turn life around."

— Leo Buscaglia

112

"Whatever you are, be a good one."

— Abraham Lincoln

113

"My recipe for life is not being afraid of myself, afraid of what I think of my opinions."

— Eartha Kitt

114

"Cheerfulness is a policy; happiness is a talent."

— Mason Cooley

115

"We emerge from the grieving process changed people, people who carry the reality of our experience and our grief forward with us into the rest of our lives."

— Christina Baldwin

116

"An excuse is worse and more terrible than a lie, for an excuse is a lie guarded."

— John Paul II

117

"To become a kinder, more living individual requires action. Yet, ironically, there is nothing specific you have to do, no prescription to follow."

— Richard Carlson

118

"Tomorrow is the most important thing in life. Comes into us at midnight very clean. It's perfect when it arrives and puts itself in our hands. It hopes we've learned something from yesterday."

— John Wayne

119

"Softly and kindly remind yourself, 'I cannot own anything.'"

— Wayne Dyer

120

"Never dwell on what you have lost, only on what you have left. Count your blessings. You'll always find plenty. Your most prized possessions are your unexpired years."

— Author Unknown

121

"Move to the rhythm of your soul and you'll never miss a beat!"

— Vicki Virk

122

"The quality of mercy is not strain'd,
It droppeth as the gentle rain from heaven."

— William Shakespeare

123

"Follow your instincts. That's where true wisdom manifests itself."

— Oprah Winfrey

124

"Life would be much easier if I had the source code."

— Author Unknown

125

"People are like stained glass windows. They sparkle and shine when the sun is out, but when the darkness sets in, their true beauty is revealed only if there is light within."

— Elisabeth Kübler-Ross

126

"A hundred men may make an encampment, but it takes a woman to make a home."

— Chinese Proverb

127

"If you want to change the world, first try to improve and bring about change within yourself. That will help change your family. From there it just gets bigger and bigger. Everything we do has some effect, some impact."

— The Dalai Lama

128

"Nobody can make you feel inferior without your permission."

— Eleanor Roosevelt

129

"Arranging a bowl of flowers in the morning can give a sense of quiet in a crowded day—like writing a poem or saying a prayer."

— Anne Morrow Lindbergh

130

"Within your heart,
Keep one still, secret spot
where dreams may go."

— Louise Driscoll

131

"Only those who dare to fail greatly can achieve greatly."

— Robert F. Kennedy

131

"A soul should always stand ajar, ready to welcome
the ecstatic experience."

— *Emily Dickinson*

132

"In the final analysis, all that we're really called on to do is accept our feelings by feeling them, and saying, 'Yes, this is what I feel.'"

— *Melody Beattie*

133

"The tragedy in life is not that it ends so soon,
but that we wait too long to begin it."

— *Author Unknown*

134

"You must learn to be still in the midst of activity
and to be vibrantly alive in repose."

— *Indira Gandhi*

135

"When there is great love, there are always miracles."

— *Willa Cather*

136

"You lose a lot of time hating people."

— Marian Anderson

137

"It is in deep solitude that I find the gentleness with which I can truly love my brothers [sisters]."

— Thomas Merton

138

"You never know when messages will fall into your lap at the exact instant you need them. The key is recognizing the messages when they appear."

— BettyClare Moffatt

139

"I am happiest when I am alone."

— Jacqueline Kennedy Onassis

140

"What is life? It is the flash of the firefly in the night. It is the breath of a buffalo in wintertime. It is the little shadow which runs across the grass and loses itself in the sunset."

— Crowfoot (Blackfoot Warrior and Orator)

141

"Our lives are like a candle in the wind."

— Carl Sandburg

142

"Our feelings are always with us, but we are too seldom with them."

— Daniel Goleman

143

"The soul never thinks without a picture."

— Aristotle

144

"Look to this Day! For it is Life, the very Life of Life."

— Kalidasa

145

"The future belongs to those who believe in the beauty of their dreams."

— Author Unknown

146

"Let us break bread together on our knees."

— African American Spiritual

147

"Courage is doing what you're afraid to do."

— Eddie Rickenbacker

148

"Go on working, freely and furiously, and you will make progress."

— Paul Gauguin

149

"I never really look for anything. What God throws my way comes.
I wake up in the morning and whichever way
God turns my feet, I go."

— Pearl Bailey

150

"I expect to pass through life but once. If therefore, there be any
kindness I can show, or any good thing I can do to any fellow being,
let me do it now, and not defer or neglect it,
as I shall not pass this way again."

— William Penn

151

"Bloom where you are planted."

— Mary Engelbreit

152

"It's better to be a lion for a day than a sheep all your life."

— Sister Elizabeth Kenny

153

"I had no idea history was being made. I was just tired of giving up."

— Rosa Parks

154

"There is nothing like returning to a place that remains unchanged to find the ways in which you yourself have altered."

— Nelson Mandela

155

"At the height of laughter, the universe is flung into a kaleidoscope of new possibilities."

— Jean Houston

156

"The kind of work we do does not make us holy, but we can make it holy."

— Meister Eckhart

157

"Joy is not in things; it is in us."

— Richard Wagner

158

"Anywhere I see suffering, that is where I want to be,
doing what I can."

— Princess Diana

159

"Blessed are those who can give without remembering,
and take without forgetting."

— Elizabeth Bibesco

160

"A mother always has to think twice,
once for herself and once for her child."

— Sophia Loren

161

"We are all here for a spell; get all the good laughs you can."

— Will Rogers

162

"Tears are the stuff of life. They are symptoms of intense feeling and the most visible symbol of what it means to be human."

— Jeffrey A. Kottler

163

"The purpose of life is a life of purpose."

— Robert Byrne

164

"Creativity can be described as letting go of uncertainties."

— Gail Sheehy

165

"Shoot for the moon. Even if you miss you'll land among the stars."

— Les Brown

166

"Become so wrapped up in something that you forget to be afraid."

— Lady Bird Johnson

167

"You can't walk alone. Many have given the illusion, but none have really walked alone. Man [woman] is not made that way. Each man [woman] is bedded in his [her] people, their history, their culture, and their values."

— Peter Abrahams

168

"Be who you are and say what you feel, because those who mind don't matter, and those who matter don't mind."

— Dr. Seuss

169

"In case of doubt, we should always lean on the side of mercy."

— Author Unknown

170

"We grow neither better nor worse as we get old, but more like ourselves."

— Bernard Baruch

171

"We are not in a position in which we have nothing to work with. We already have capacities, talents, direction, missions, calling."

— Abraham Maslow

172

"Life is a progress, not a station."

— Ralph Waldo Emerson

173

"I restore myself when I'm alone. A career is born in public; talent in privacy."

— Marilyn Monroe

174

"Your talent is God's gift to you. What you do with it is your gift back to God."

— Leo Buscaglia

175

"Some of us think holding on makes us strong; but sometimes it is letting go."

— Hermann Hesse

176

"Where there is sorrow there is holy ground."

— Oscar Wilde

177

"May your joys be as deep as the ocean,
your sorrows as light as its foam."

— Author Unknown

178

"Ain't no man can avoid being born average,
but ain't no man got to be common."

— Satchel Paige

179

"Learn to get in touch with the silence within yourself and know that everything in this life has purpose."

— Elisabeth Kübler-Ross

180

"No one has ever become poor by giving."

— Anne Frank

181

"The comforter's head never aches."

— Italian Proverb

182

"People see God every day; they just don't recognize Him."

— Pearl Bailey

183

"We may take something like a star,
To stay our minds on and be staid."

— Robert Frost

184

"When we do the best we can, we never know what miracle is wrought in our life, or the life of another."

— Helen Keller

185

"Meditation is from moment to moment. The eyes see, the ears hear. The organs function. There is no interiorsation, no concentration, no introversion, no withdrawing of the senses. Don't go into the old habits of withdrawal. Go in the directionless expansion, the spaceless space."

— Jean Klein

186

"The human voice can never reach the distance that is covered by the still small voice of conscience."

— Mahatma Gandhi

187

"Every life has a measure of sorrow, and sometimes this is what awakens us."

— Steven Tyler

188

"Grief is a wound that needs attention in order to heal."

— Judy Tatelbaum

189

"Motherhood has a very humanizing effect. Everything gets reduced to essentials."

— Meryl Streep

189

"Never play peek-a-boo with a child on a long plane trip. There's no end to the game. Finally I grabbed him by the bib and said, 'Look, it's always gonna be me!'"

— Rita Rudner

190

"If you have talent, use it in every way possible. Don't hoard it. Don't dole it out like a miser. Spend it lavishly like a millionaire intent on going broke."

— Brendan Francis Behan

191

"In our era, the road to holiness necessarily passes through the world of action."

— Dag Hammarskjöld

192

"Happiness depends on ourselves."

— Aristotle

193

"Giving liberates the soul of the giver."

— Maya Angelou

194

"Certainly we have demands on our time, responsibilities that must be met and jobs that must be done. But when we begin to treat each moment as the special gift it is, honoring it by giving it our full attention before we move on to the next, then every day becomes a day well spent and every life becomes a celebration."

— Dominique Glocheux

195

"Happiness is a matter of one's most ordinary, everyday mode of consciousness being busy and lively and unconcerned with self."

— Iris Murdoch

196

"Do thou thy task and leave the rest to God."

— Lewis Carroll

197

"Faith means loving with uncertainty—feeling your way through life, letting your heart guide you like a lantern in the dark."

— Dan Millman

198

"What if the healing of the world utterly depends on the ten thousand invisible kindnesses we offer simply and quietly throughout the pilgrimage of each human life?"

— Author Unknown

199

"Other things may change us, but we start and end with family."

— Anthony Brandt

200

"There is in every true woman's heart a spark of heavenly fire, which lies dormant in the broad daylight of prosperity; but which kindles up, and beams and blazes in the dark hour of adversity."

— Washington Irving

201

"It takes two to make peace."

— John F. Kennedy

203

"Accepting the hard realities in your own life that you cannot change will free you to examine and embrace the choices that you do have."

— Harriet B. Braiker

204

"Our feelings are our most genuine path to knowledge."

— Audre Lorde

205

"So many gods, so many creeds, so many paths that wind and wind, while just the art of being kind is all the sad world needs."

— Ella Wheeler Wilcox

206

"By having a reverence for life we enter a spiritual relation with the world. By practicing reverence for life we become good, deep, and alive."

— Albert Schweitzer

207

"Religion is what you do when the sermon is over."

—Author Unknown

208

"The rhythm of your heartbeat assures and ensures constant inflowing and outflowing of good. The more you tend your flame and tender it to others, the more tenderness you have to give. The more love you give, the more you perceive that love is always there . . ."

—BettyClare Moffatt

209

"Word I was in my life alone,
Word I had no one left but God."

—Robert Frost

210

"No man or woman of the humblest sort can really be strong, gentle and good, without the world being better for it, without somebody being helped and comforted by the very existence of that goodness."

—Alan Alda

211

"Spirituality is the domain of awareness."

— Deepak Chopra

212

"There will come a time when you believe everything is finished. That will be the beginning."

— Louis L'Amour

213

"You can't get mad at somebody who makes you laugh— it's as simple as that."

— Jay Leno

214

"Swallow your pride occasionally, it's non-fattening!"

— Author Unknown

215

"I define joy as a sustained sense of well-being and internal peace— a connection to what matters."

— Oprah Winfrey

216

"I am comforted by life's stability, by earth's unchangeableness. What has seemed new and frightening assumes its place in the unfolding of knowledge."

— Pearl S. Buck

217

"Be not afraid of life. Believe that life is worth living, and your belief will help you create the fact."

— William James

218

"You cannot run away from weakness; you must some time fight it out or perish; and if that be soon, why not now, and where do you stand?"

— Robert Louis Stevenson

219

"The depth of your compassion lies in your ability to forgive yourself."

— Mark Graham

220

"If we don't change, we don't grow. If we don't grow, we are not really living. Growth demands a temporary surrender of security."

— Gail Sheehy

221

"Joy is a light that fills you with hope and faith and love."

— Adela Rogers St. Johns

222

"Unlike seeing, where one can look away, one cannot 'hear away' but must listen . . . hearing implies already belonging together in such a manner that one is claimed by what is being said."

— Hans-Georg Gadamer

223

"Without craftsmanship, inspiration is a mere reed shaken in the wind."

— Johannes Brahms

224

"In thought, faith
In word, wisdom
In deed, courage
In life, service."

— Author Unknown

225

"You've achieved success in your field when you don't know whether what you're doing is work or play."

— Warren Beatty

226

"The best way out of a problem is through it."

— Author Unknown

227

"All of us have seen good come out of disaster . . . the blessing in disguise. When you expect good to come from negativity, it will. What you think about, you bring about."

— Joyce Duco

228

"God expects but one thing of you, and that is you should come out of yourself in so far as you are a created being and let God be God in you."

— Meister Eckhart

229

"The soul gives us resilience—an essential quality since we constantly have to rebound from hardship."

— Wynton Marsalis

230

"The only time my prayers aren't answered is on the golf course."

— Billy Graham

231

"It is only when we truly know and understand that we have a limited time on earth and that we have no way of knowing when our time is up that we begin to live each day to the fullest, as if it were the only one we had."

— *Elisabeth Kübler-Ross*

232

"Love has nothing to do with what you are expecting to get— only what you are expecting to give."

— *Katharine Hepburn*

233

"Sometimes life has a way of putting us on our backs in order to force us to look up."

— *Charles L. Allen*

234

"I don't wait for moods. You accomplish nothing if you do that. Your mind must know it has to get down to work."

— *Pearl S. Buck*

235

"Darkness cannot drive out darkness, only light can do that. Hate cannot drive out hate; only love can do that."

— *Martin Luther King Jr.*

236

"If God wanted us to live in a permissive society he would have given us Ten Suggestions and not Ten Commandments."

— Zig Ziglar

237

"As the family goes, so goes the nation and so goes the world in which we live."

— John Paul II

238

"One single idea can change your life. Open your eyes and prick up your ears. It may appear at any time, without making any noise or when you don't see it coming."

— Dominique Glocheux

239

"No pessimist ever discovered the secrets of the stars, or sailed to an uncharted land, or opened a new heaven to the horizon of the spirit."

— Helen Keller

240

"'Tis grace hath brought me safe thus far, and grace will lead me home."

— John Newton

241

"The soul is not a physical entity, but instead refers to everything about us that is not physical— our values, memories, identity, sense of humor. Since the soul represents the parts of the human being that are not physical, it cannot get sick, it cannot die, it cannot disappear. In short, the soul is immortal."

— Harold Kushner

242

"Abundance is not something we acquire.
It is something we tune into."

— Wayne Dyer

243

"Teach me to feel another's woe
To hide the fault I see,
That mercy I to others show,
That mercy show to me."

— Alexander Pope

244

"What we call the secret of happiness is no more a secret than your willingness to choose life."

— Leo Buscaglia

245

"Don't worry about the world coming to an end today.
It's already tomorrow in Australia."

— Charles M. Schulz

246

"Benedictine monks use the hourly chimes of a clock to remind them to pause and pray 'the hour of prayer.' If you have a watch or cell phone with an alarm, you could do the same."

— Rick Warren

247

"Hide not your talents, they for use were made.
What's a sun-dial in the shade?"

— Benjamin Franklin

248

"Give to yourself before giving to others.
You will have more to give."

— Dominique Glocheux

249

"Well-timed, sincere words of praise are absolutely free and worth a fortune."

— Sam Walton

250

"We're all familiar with a blessing in disguise. What is less commonly appreciated is the disguise in many a blessing."

— *Mardy Grothe*

251

"Changes are not predictable, but to deny them is to be an accomplice to one's own unnecessary vegetation."

— *Gail Sheehy*

252

"Sometimes it only takes a word, a phrase, a drumbeat, a circle, a song, a room full of women in harmony together, to remind us of all that we are."

— *BettyClare Moffatt*

253

"Stand up and walk out of your history."

— *Phil McGraw*

254

"It's not until you become a mother that your judgment slowly turns to compassion and understanding."

— *Erma Bombeck*

255

"Imagination is the highest kite one can fly."

– Lauren Bacall

256

"Everything in life that we really accept undergoes a change."

– Katherine Mansfield

257

"A hero is an ordinary individual who finds the strength to persevere and endure in spite of overwhelming obstacles."

– Christopher Reeve

258

"All makers must leave room for the acts of the spirit. But they have to work hard and carefully and wait patiently to deserve them."

– Ursula K. Le Guin

259

"The hardest arithmetic to master is that which enables us to count our blessings."

– Eric Hoffer

260

"Everyone of us needs to be valued. Everyone has the potential to give something back."

— *Princess Diana*

261

"I took a deep breath and listened to the old bray of my heart. I am. I am. I am."

— *Sylvia Plath*

262

"Life is the greatest bargain; we get it for nothing."

— *Yiddish Proverb*

263

"You know, you don't have to look like everybody else to be acceptable and to feel acceptable."

— *Fred Rogers*

264

"Emotional awareness starts with attunement to the stream of feeling that is a constant presence in all of us and with a recognition of how these emotions shape what we perceive, think, and do."

— *Daniel Goleman*

265

"The final forming of a person's character lies in their own hands."

— Anne Frank

266

"Change is the constant and we are constantly in change."

— Christina Baldwin

267

"A life that doesn't have a definite plan is likely to become driftwood."

— David Sarnoff

268

"There is nothing wrong with wanting to be alone."

— Robert Veniga

269

"Everybody's a teacher if you listen."

— Doris Roberts

270

"Forgiveness is an act of imagination. It dares you to imagine a better future, one that is based on the blessed possibility that your hurt will not be the final word on the matter. It challenges you to give up on your destructive thoughts about the situation and believe in the possibility of a better future. It builds confidence that you can survive the pain and grow from it."

— Larry James

271

"All you really need is love, but a little chocolate now and then doesn't hurt."

— Charles M. Schulz

272

"Poems are made by fools like me,
But only God can make a tree."

— Joyce Kilmer

273

"To forgive yourself is to set yourself free."

— Ruby Bridges Hall

274

"Letting your mind play is the best way to solve problems."

— Bill Watterson

275

"Joy runs deeper than despair."

– Corrie Ten Boom

276

"Think twice and pray three times before punishing a child."

– Maltbie D. Babcock

277

"People travel to wonder at the height of the mountains,
at the huge waves of the seas, at the long course of the rivers,
at the vast compass of the ocean,
at the circular motion of the stars,
and yet they pass by themselves without wondering."

– St. Augustine

278

"There is no grief which time does not lessen and soften."

– Cicero

279

"Humor must have its background of seriousness.
Without this contact there comes none of that incongruity
which is the mainspring of laughter."

– Max Beerbohm

280

"Wisdom and virtue are like the two wheels of a cart."

— Japanese Proverb

281

"It is often easier to fight for principles than to live up to them."

— Adlai Stevenson

282

"The wish to pray is a prayer itself."

— George Bernanos

283

"Because God has so much strength and power, He can supply us with the strength we need when we face challenges that exceed our human capacities."

— Harold Kushner

284

"We will surely get to our destination if we join hands."

— Aung San Suu Kyi

285

"Think of yourself as an incandescent power, illuminated and perhaps forever talked to by God and his messengers."

– Brenda Ueland

286

"The habit of giving only enhances the desire to give."

– Walt Whitman

287

"Unity is strength . . . when there is teamwork and collaboration, wonderful things can be achieved."

– Mattie Stepanek

288

"It is this belief in a power larger than myself and other than myself which allows me to venture into the unknown and even the unknowable."

– Maya Angelou

289

"Do not weep; do not wax indignant. Understand."

– Baruch Spinoza

290

"Life is either a daring adventure or nothing. To keep our faces toward change and behave like free spirits in the presence of fate is strength undefeatable."

— Helen Keller

291

"With a good conscience our only sure reward, with history the final judge of our deeds, let us go forth to lead the land we love, asking His blessing and His help, but knowing that here on earth God's work must be truly our own."

— John F. Kennedy

292

"He [she] who laughs, lasts."

— Mary Pettibone Poole

293

"I'm always thinking about creating. My future starts when I wake up every morning . Every day I find something creative to do with my life."

— Miles Davis

295

"The greatest prayer is patience."

— Buddha

296

"Some luck lies in not getting what you thought you wanted but getting what you have, which once you have got it you may be smart enough to see is what you would have wanted had you known."

— Garrison Keillor

297

"Justice is a temporary thing that must at last come to an end; but the conscience is eternal and will never die."

— Martin Luther

298

"Take the time to come home to yourself every day."

— Robin Casarjian

299

"Real generosity toward the future lies in giving all to the present."

— Albert Camus

300

"Anyone who keeps the ability to see a beautiful world never grows old."

— Franz Kafka

301

"Prayer is not an old woman's idle amusement. Properly understood and applied, it is the most potent instrument of action."

— Mahatma Gandhi

302

"Let parents bequeath to their children not riches but the spirit of reverence."

— Plato

303

"Gratitude makes sense of our past, peace for today, and creates a vision for tomorrow."

— Melody Beattie

304

"Stop worrying about the potholes in the road and celebrate the journey!"

— Barbara Hoffman

305

"You grow up the day you have your first real laugh, at yourself."

— Ethel Barrymore

306

"We must accept the final disappointment,
but never lose infinite hope."

— Martin Luther King, Jr.

307

"True silence is the rest of the mind, and is to the spirit what sleep is to the body, nourishment and refreshment."

— William Penn

308

"Do not be afraid of life. Believe that life is worth living, and your belief will help you create the fact."

— William James

309

"If you want a thing done well, get a couple of old broads to do it."

— Bette Davis

310

"A blessed thing it is for any man or woman to have a friend, one human soul whom we can trust utterly, who knows the best and worse of us, and loves us in spite of our faults."

— Charles Kingsley

311

"Growth itself contains a germ of happiness."

— Pearl S. Buck

312

"To be old is a glorious thing when one has not unlearned what it means to begin."

— Martin Buber

313

"Some pursue happiness, others create it."

— Author Unknown

314

"Testing oneself is best done when done alone."

— Jimmy Carter

315

"I define comfort as self-acceptance when we finally learn that self-care begins and ends with ourselves, we no longer demand sustenance and happiness from others."

— Jennifer Louden

316

"In three words I can summarize everything I've learned about life: It goes on."

— *Robert Frost*

317

"Pray, and let God worry."

— *Martin Luther*

318

"All the art of living lies in a fine mingling of letting go and holding on."

— *Havelock Ellis*

319

"Life is not easy for any of us. But what of that? We must have perseverance and above all confidence in ourselves. We must believe that we are gifted for something and that this thing must be attained."

— *Marie Curie*

320

"Don't spend your precious time asking, 'Why isn't the world a better place?' It will only be time wasted. The question to ask is, 'How can I make it better?'"

— *Leo Buscaglia*

321

"The mere sense of living is joy enough."

— Emily Dickinson

322

"Life affords no greater responsibility, no greater privilege, than the raising of the next generation."

— C. Everett Koop

323

"Joys are our wings, sorrows our spurs."

— Jean Paul

324

"In everyone's life at some time, our inner fire goes out. It is then burst into flame by an encounter with another human being. We should all be grateful for these people who rekindle the human spirit."

— Albert Schweitzer

325

"Life is just a chance to grow a soul."

— A. Powell Davies

326

"Empathy begins inside."

— Daniel Goleman

327

"A problem is a chance for you to do your best."

— Duke Ellington

328

"There are people who put their dreams in a little box and say,
'Yes, I've got dreams, of course I've got dreams.'
Then they put the box away and bring it out once in awhile
and look at it, and yep, they're still there."

— Erma Bombeck

329

"Adventure is not outside of man [woman]; it is within."

— David Grayson

330

"Those who contemplate the beauty of the earth find reserves
of strength that will endure as long as life lasts."

— Rachael Carlson

331

"For fast-acting relief, try slowing down."

— Lily Tomlin

332

"The soul would have no rainbow had the eyes no tears."

— John Vance Cheney

333

"Never doubt that a small group of thoughtful, committed people can change the world. Indeed, it is the only thing that ever has."

— Margaret Mead

334

"Turn your wounds into wisdom."

— Oprah Winfrey

335

"Kind words can be short and easy to speak,
but their echoes are truly endless."

— Mother Teresa

336

"Making mistakes simply means you are learning faster."

— Weston H. Agor

337

"Anger in its time and place,
May assume a kind of grace."

— Charles and Mary Lamb

338

"The time you enjoy wasting is not wasted time."

— Bertrand Russell

339

"If you want more, you have to require more for yourself."

— Phil McGraw

340

"Blessed is the man [woman] who has found his [her] work;
let him [her] ask no other blessedness."

— Thomas Carlyle

341

"The work praises the man [woman]."

— Irish Proverb

342

"An ounce of action is worth a ton of theory."

— Fredrich Engels

343

"A straight path never leads anywhere except to the objective."

— André Gide

344

"One can endure sorrow alone, but it takes two to be glad."

— Elbert Hubbard

345

"Loving someone is setting them free, letting them go."

— Kate Winslet

346

"God gives no linen, but flax to spin."

— German Proverb

347

"No kind action ever stops with itself. One kind action leads to another. Good example is followed. A single act of kindness throws out roots in all directions, and the roots spring up and make new trees. The greatest work that kindness does to others is that it makes them kind to themselves."

— Amelia Earhart

348

"You don't have to be noisy to be effective."

— Philip Crosby

349

"I dwell in possibility."

— Emily Dickinson

350

"I have found that if you love life, life will love you back."

— Arthur Rubinstein

351

"Never work just for money or for power. They won't save your soul or help you sleep at night."

— Marian Wright Edelman

352

"Creativity comes from trust. Trust your instincts. And never hope more than you work."

— Rita Mae Brown

353

"Only the person who has faith in himself [herself] is able to be faithful to others."

— *Erich Fromm*

354

"Laughter is the most direct route to God . . . filling our heads with Light as we go."

— *Henry Miller*

355

"The art of being wise is the act of knowing what to overlook."

— *William James*

356

"Hitch your wagon to a star."

— *Ralph Waldo Emerson*

357

"No one can drive us crazy unless we give them the keys."

— *Doug Horton*

358

"All that we love deeply becomes part of us."

— *Helen Keller*

359

"Self-image sets the boundaries of individual accomplishments."

— Maxwell Maltz

360

"When I do good, I feel good. When I do bad, I feel bad.
And that's my religion."

— Abraham Lincoln

361

"We all start out with no discipline, no patience, no perseverance, no determination. We all start out at zero. People say, 'You have talent.' No, the gift is to realize that we all start out even. Whether we messed up or put our best foot forward, with these four qualities, we take care of our mental, physical, and spiritual health each day. Am I the best in the world? No.
The question is: 'Am I the best I can be?'"

— Edward James Olmos

362

"My mind to me a kingdom is; such perfect joy therein I find."

— Edward Dyer

363

"All of us deserve happiness or none of us does."

— Mary Gordon

364

"Daily we choose. Complaining or courage. Dependency or interdependency. Resentment or acceptance. Creator or destroyer. Integrity or disgust. It's time for you to choose."

— BettyClare Moffatt

365

"I wouldn't trade anything for my story now."

— Maya Angelou

Part 6

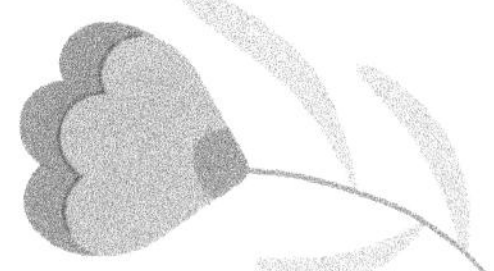

Nurturing Yourself

Inspiring as they may be, reading a bunch of quotes doesn't help much unless you do something with them. That's why I wrote this part. In an ideal situation, you would do something for yourself every day, but women tend not to do that. Often, we care for others before we care for ourselves. Then too, we come up with a variety of excuses for our behavior.

I don't have time to care for myself.

Caring for ________ *(fill in the blank)* is my priority now.

After things calm down, I'll take better care of myself.

Each statement is partially true, but you can't help others unless you take care of yourself first. You are worthy of self-care. If you can't nurture yourself daily, you may be able to do it once a week. Even small things, such as meeting a friend for coffee, or reading for pleasure, or getting a haircut, can be helpful.

Please make this promise: *I will nurture myself today.* Making a promise is like planting a seed. Personal growth may not happen as quickly as a tiny shoot peeking through the soil, yet growth will happen. Indeed, the pledge can have a huge impact on your life. As time passes, you will look, feel, and act happier. You become more aware of yourself and your life.

What's more, this promise can enrich your soul.

I'm 90 years old and some of the suggestions in this section come from my experience. Other suggestions come from the quotes themselves. Discovering quote-related ideas was surprising and fun. Of course, you will have your own ideas based on your personality, education, and experience.

When I chose these points, I focused on "freebies," ways of nurturing yourself that had little or no cost to them. Obvious ideas—going to church or synagogue, spending time with a loving family, taking care of a beloved pet—aren't on this list because I thought you probably do them already.

These ideas allow for options. "Do something to make your home more comfortable," is an example. What might this entail? You could straighten a messy desk, rearrange furniture, or buy a small plant, etc. What you do with these ideas is up to you. You may wish to put a checkmark next to the points that seem workable or highlight them for easy access.

Part 7

Ideas for Nurturing Yourself

When I was in my mid-fifties I thought, as I became older, I would nurture myself automatically. After all, I had many different experiences, made many decisions, and responded to life-changing events. But my idea turned out to be false because life keeps sending us surprises.

Once I realized this, I made self-nurturing a daily priority. This included saying "no," which used to be hard for me. Now I say "no" easily and kindly, and follow it with a one-sentence explanation.

One of the most self-nurturing steps I have taken was not saying "sorry" automatically. All too often, I said I was sorry when I had nothing to be sorry about. As a friend suggested, "We have to stop apologizing and saying we're sorry when it's not necessary." I agree wholeheartedly. Unless I'm genuinely sorry, I avoid the word.

With each passing year, I learn more about nurturing and what it entails. The ideas on the following pages come from learning and life experience. (Mostly experience.) "Be honest with yourself" is one of my favorites and, believe me, I practice it. You may wish to highlight or put a checkmark by the ideas that appeal to you.

Nurture yourself as though you are the most precious thing in your life. Because you are!

Write a quote on a sticky note, put it in your pocket, and read it several times during the day.

Share your favorite quotes with other women.

Post a favorite quote on the refrigerator door where you will see it often.

Think about what makes this day special.

Do something kind for a friend.

Sing while you're cleaning or washing the dishes.

Look for small, sacred things today.

Laugh whenever you can.

Enjoy a few quiet, solitary moments. You deserve them.

Listen to soothing music.

Make a list of what you learn from painful feelings.

Keep track of your own quotes in a computer file or notebook.

Try something new today, a hobby, recipe, or sport.

Trust your feelings.

Never give up.

Think of trouble as an opportunity in work clothes.

Be honest with yourself.

Let nature restore and energize you.

As soon as you wake up, name five friends who have helped you.

Help a child or children today.

Acknowledge your mistakes and accomplishments.

Counter a negative thought with a positive one.

Name your feelings if you can.

Stop what you're doing and say a short, simple prayer.

Think of birthdays as chances to learn more.

Continue to learn.

Remember that silence can be stronger than words.

Be willing to let go when necessary.

Practice mindfulness often.

Acknowledge your fears and plan for them.

Remind yourself that you can't fix everything.

Notice the rhythm of your life.

Do something to make your home more comfortable.

Accept your feelings and tell yourself, "This is how I feel."

Picture your dreams in your mind.

Keep at it until you make progress.

Be proud of the work you do.

Think of tears as a language all their own.

Access the natural creativity within you.

Email a friend you haven't seen in some time.

Just be yourself.

Give to others when you can.

Share your talents; they were given to you for a reason.

Remember that happiness is a choice.

Let go of pride if it will make things better.

Access the wellspring of strength inside you.

Praise someone with a short, genuine compliment.

Disagree in a courteous, respectful way.

Calm yourself with diaphragm breathing.

Instead of thinking of a reply, be an active listener.

Forgive others and yourself.

Say “I love you” every day.

The word “nurture” means different things to different people. We nurture ourselves in different ways, and what nurtures you may not nurture me. My publisher has her own ways of nurturing herself and here’s her list:

Take a warm bath and play relaxing music in the background.

Spend time walking in nature.

Get a massage.

Spend a day at a spa being pampered.

If you live near a hot springs, treat yourself to a soak in the mineral water.

Find a relaxing nail salon and get a manicure and pedicure.

Pick up your favorite coffee or tea from a local coffee shop (or bring your own) and go to a nearby park to enjoy nature and some people watching.

Take a drive in a wooded area and take in the beauty and comfort of nature.

Play your favorite music while you do household chores.

In the early morning, sit on your balcony, porch, patio, etc. with a cup of tea or coffee and watch the world wake up.

Play sleep music as you unwind and get ready for sleep.

Part 8

Final Thoughts

The idea of singing while you're cleaning or doing dishes comes from me. I sing all the time. When I hear music in a grocery store, I sing along with it, much to my daughters' embarrassment. Years ago, my two daughters came to the grocery store with me, and when I heard the background music I began to sing.

"Mom, just because you know the song doesn't mean you sing it," my younger daughter said.

"I know," I answered. "But I can't help myself."

I took voice lessons, sang at Carnegie Recital Hall, shows, weddings, and church services. Now that I live alone, I sing in the shower, sing when I'm working at the computer, and sing in the elevator. For me, singing is a spiritual experience.

Writing is also a spiritual experience for me and has been for more than 50 years. Before I begin to write, I sit at my computer, close my eyes, and meditate for a few minutes. Then I say a short prayer.

Spirit of Life and God of my heart,
Let me be helpful,
Let me be clear,
Let the words come
From my soul.

Writing goes better when I do this. Maybe saying a short prayer relaxes me. Then too, prayer is a link to spirituality.

When it comes to spirituality, I nurture myself in several ways. At this age and stage of life, I know I need quiet time each day, uninterrupted hours to reflect on my life, my health, and my family. I usually read for pleasure during this time. If I don't have quiet time, I become Mrs. Grumpy, but that doesn't last long, thank goodness.

I've nurtured myself through happy and profoundly sad times.

Being with family members and friends helped tremendously. Writing self-help books helped me and helped readers. Because I've nurtured my spirituality for so long, I don't need reminders. However, you may wish to put "Nurturing Time" on your calendar.

Please continue to nurture yourself because there's only one YOU in all the world. You are special.

About the Author

Harriet Hodgson has been an independent journalist for forty-six years. She has a BS in Early Childhood Education from Wheelock College of Education and Human Development at Boston University, an MA in Art Education from the University of Minnesota and is a certified art therapy coach.

A prolific writer, Hodgson is the author of forty-six books and hundreds of online and print articles. Many of her books have won awards.

All of Hodgson's writing comes from experience, and she has shared her experiences on more than 190 radio talk shows, including CBS Radio, and dozens of television programs/stations, including CNN. A popular speaker, Hodgson has given presentations at nursing, Alzheimer's, hospice, public health, and grief conferences.

Her work is cited in Who's Who of American Women, World Who's Who of Women and other directories. Hodgson lives in Rochester, Minnesota. Visit www.harriethodgson.net for more information about this busy author, speaker, community volunteer, doodle artist, grandmother, and great-grandmother.

More Books by Harriet Hodgson

from WriteLife Publishing

Winning: A Story of Grief and Renewal
Foreword Reviews 2023 Book of the Year Award

Grief Doodling: Bringing Back Your Smiles
Foreword Reviews 2021 Book of the Year Award, 2021 Firebird Book Award Winner

Affirmations for Family Caregivers

A Journal for Family Caregivers

The Grandma Force: How Grandmothers are Changing Families, Grandchildren, and Themselves
Book Excellence Award Winner, Elite Choice Awards, Living Now Awards Silver Medal

So, You're Raising Your Grandkids: Tested Tips, Research, and Real-Life Stories to Make Your Life Easier
2018 New Apple Book Awards Winner, Grand Prize Rave Reviews Book Club International Book Awards

Ready, Set, Lead!, with coauthor Kathy Kasten
2022 Firebird Book Award Winner

Daisy a Day: Hope for a Grieving Heart
2022 Firebird Book Award Winner

Grief in Your Words: How Writing Helps You Heal
2025 Firebird Book Award Winner